Clever COGZ
THE BOOK OF
FLYING MACHINES

By Neil Clark

Quarto is the authority on a wide range of topics.

Quarto educates, entertains and enriches the lives of
our readers—enthusiasts and lovers of hands-on living.

www.quartoknows.com

Author & Illustrator: Neil Clark
Consultant: Oliver Green
Editor: Harriet Stone
Designer: Sarah Chapman-Suire

This edition first published in 2019
by QEB Publishing,
an imprint of The Quarto Group.
26391 Crown Valley Parkway, Suite 220
Mission Viejo, CA 92691, USA
T: +1 949 380 7510
F: +1 949 380 7575
www.QuartoKnows.com

A CIP record for this book is available from
the Library of Congress.

ISBN 978 0 7112 4344 6

Manufactured in Shenzhen, China PP092019

9 8 7 6 5 4 3 2 1

MIX
Paper from
responsible sources
FSC® C001701

CONTENTS

Flying Machines

Flying machines, or aircraft, are used to carry people and objects through the air. People have been making aircraft for over two hundred years. There are lots of different types. Look up at the sky with Cogz. What aircraft can you see?

Flying machines are air-mazing. I can't wait to learn more!

Hot Air Balloon

These aircraft are filled with hot air to make them float. Learn more on page 14.

Jumbo Jet

These airplanes are gigantic! Learn more about jumbo jets on page 18.

This is called
wing-walking!
wahoo!

Biplane
Airplanes come in all shapes
and sizes. Biplanes have
two pairs of wings.

Airship
Airships are big aircraft filled
with gas. They were the first
powered and controllable aircraft.

This autogyro is
like a mini helicopter.
Learn about helicopters
on page 16.

Fighter Plane
These planes can twist and turn very
fast! Learn about a fighter plane called
a Spitfire on page 12.

Airplanes

An airplane is a type of aircraft powered by an engine. They are made of metal. Thousands of airplanes fly every day. Have you ever been in one? An airplane is made from lots of clever parts. Let's take a closer look...

tail

fin

The **rudder** steers the plane left or right. The pilot uses pedals to move the rudder.

Every airplane needs **wings** so it can fly. Find out how wings work on page 8.

The fuel tank contains a special kind of gasoline called jet fuel. Without fuel, a plane wouldn't have the energy to GO!

fuel tank

A bit like me if I haven't had any breakfast!

N

The main body of an aircraft is called the **fuselage**. It holds the people or objects that the plane is carrying.

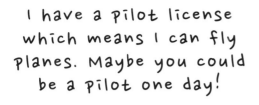
I have a pilot license which means I can fly planes. Maybe you could be a pilot one day!

Propellers spin to keep an airplane moving forward. Turn to page 10 to learn more!

fuselage

cockpit

engine

These strong **wheels** are needed for a smooth takeoff and a safe landing.

The Wright brothers flew the very first airplane in 1903.

7

Wings

Wings are a very important part of an airplane. These heavy machines wouldn't get off the ground without wings. So how do they work? Clever Cogz knows the answer.

Lift is the force that keeps an aircraft in the air.

Wing Shape

As the plane moves forward, air flows past the wings. The air travels faster over the top than it does underneath. The slow-moving air under the wing creates a force called lift.

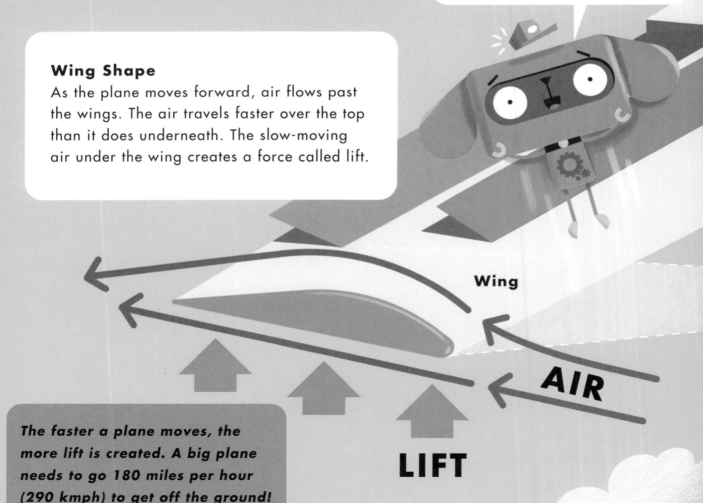

Wing

AIR

LIFT

The faster a plane moves, the more lift is created. A big plane needs to go 180 miles per hour (290 kmph) to get off the ground!

Wing Parts

Airplane wings have moving panels that work together to control the speed and direction of the plane.

When a plane lands on the runway the **spoilers** are lifted up. This slows the plane down and keeps it safely on the ground.

These **flaps** fold downward to create more lift during takeoff.

The **ailerons** move up and down to help turn the plane left or right.

What? Not mice?

Birds, insects, and bats are the only animals that use wings to fly.

Propellers

We know that wings can lift an airplane up, but a plane also needs to move forward to stay in the air. Propellers and jet engines move a plane forward in two different ways.

Propellers are cool!

Airplane fans

Have you ever stood in front of a fan to cool down? Propellers work in a similar way, moving the air around them.

1) The engine powers the propeller.

2) The propeller spins very fast.

I'm getting dizzy just thinking about this.

3) Air moves over the blades and pulls the plane forward. This is called thrust.

AIR

Jet Engines

Jet engines are a lot more powerful than propellers. They work by moving air through a metal tube and blasting hot gases out the other end.

Let's take a look inside a jet engine!

AIR

1) Air is sucked in by a giant fan.

2) The air mixes with fuel.

3) The mixture is burned.

4) Very hot gases are forced out the back of the engine...BLAST!

5) This blast of gas creates thrust, which moves the plane forward.

Spitfire

The Spitfire is a fighter plane. It helped Britain win many battles in World War 2. There were over 20,000 built during the war. Now there are only 50 that still work.

Pilots communicated with people on the ground using radio signals picked up by the **aerial mast**.

Metal Machine

In the 1920s, scientists and engineers found new ways of using metal to make airplanes safer and stronger.

Camouflage

Many fighter planes are painted to make them hard to spot. Camouflage is a clever way of blending in with the surroundings. Bolt is wearing camouflage too. Can you spot him?

Geronimo!

Parachute Protection

If a plane was hit during a battle, the pilot would leap out of the aircraft and use their parachute to float safely to the ground.

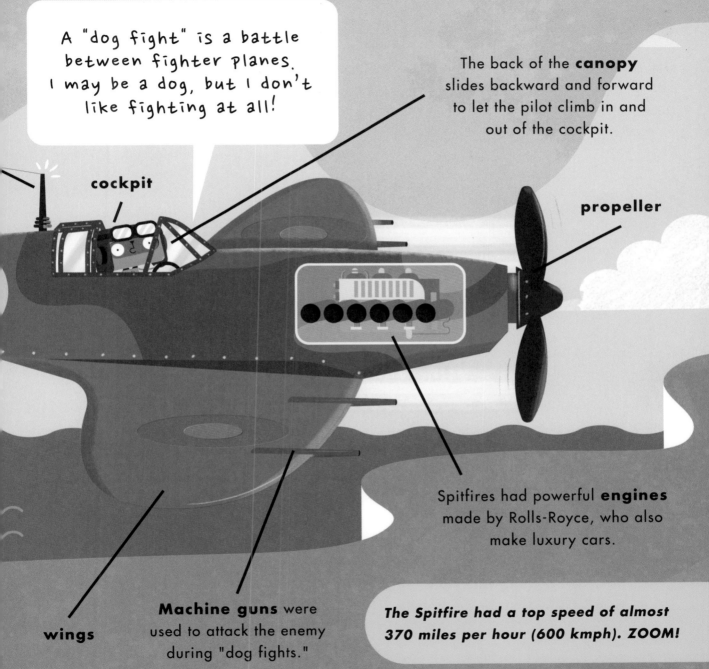

A "dog fight" is a battle between fighter planes. I may be a dog, but I don't like fighting at all!

The back of the **canopy** slides backward and forward to let the pilot climb in and out of the cockpit.

cockpit

propeller

Spitfires had powerful **engines** made by Rolls-Royce, who also make luxury cars.

Machine guns were used to attack the enemy during "dog fights."

wings

The Spitfire had a top speed of almost 370 miles per hour (600 kmph). ZOOM!

13

Hot Air Balloon

Up, up and away! Have you ever seen a hot air balloon up in the sky? These colorful balloons look magical as they float overhead. There must be something really special inside to keep them afloat...

Actually, no! It's just air. The same air that we breathe, except it has been heated up.

1) The pilot uses burners to blast hot air into the balloon.

2) When air is heated it expands and spreads out. This makes it lighter than the cold air around it, so it rises up!

This **vent** is used to let hot air escape. This makes the balloon slowly float back down.

The balloon's fabric **envelope** is made from nylon, the same material as your umbrella.

How do you steer this thing?

You can't! we travel whichever way the wind is blowing!

The pilot and passengers stand in the **basket**. A big balloon can carry over 880 pounds (400 kg). That's the same as six people.

The **burners** light the fuel to create a flame. The bigger the flame, the faster the balloon rises!

Flying with fire can be dangerous! Balloons have a **fire extinguisher** on board.

Gas tanks hold the fuel that powers the burners.

Helicopter

The helicopter is an exciting invention. It is one of the only machines that can take off and land without a run-up. Helicopters can fly up, down, sideways, backward, and can even hover in midair like a bumble bee. This makes them very useful.

Without a **tail rotor** the helicopter would spin out of control.

Oh no! Nutty's boat is leaking! Helicopters are perfect for rescuing people in hard-to-reach places.

Early Helicopters

A very clever man named Leonardo da Vinci designed a helicopter in the 1400s. Genius! The first working helicopter wasn't built until hundreds of years later, in 1938.

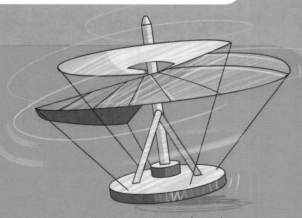

Leonardo da Vinci's Airscrew helicopter

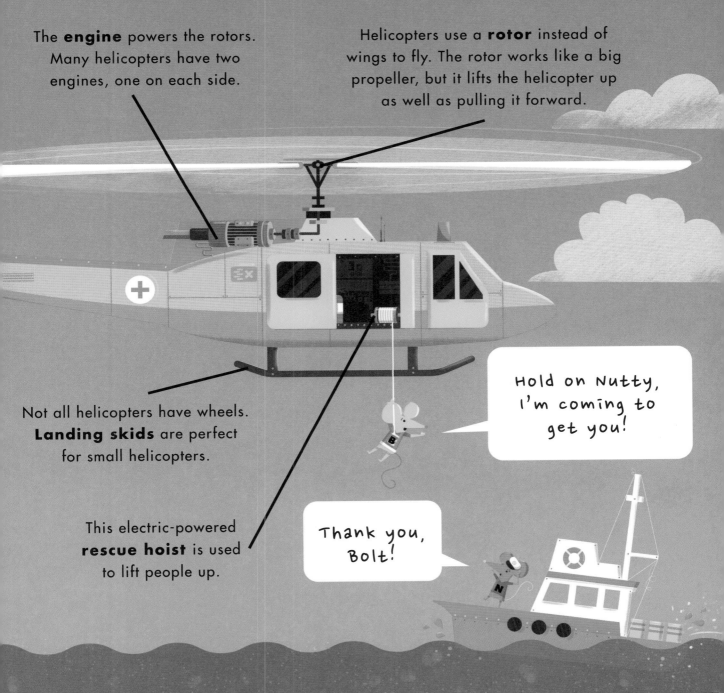

Jumbo Jet

Cogz and his friend Connie are going on vacation. They will be flying in a jumbo jet! A jumbo jet is a giant airplane used to transport people and cargo all over the world.

Boeing 747

This jumbo jet is called a Boeing 747. The first one was built in the USA in 1969. The factory it was made in is the biggest building in the world!

There are 500 **seats** for the passengers, and there's still room for all their luggage!

This airplane is so big that I can't find Nutty and Bolt. Can you spot them?

Lots of **fuel tanks** are hidden around the plane, including in the wings.

Jumbo sized

The Boeing 747 is over 230 feet (70 m) long. That's longer than two blue whales! It can fly at up to 570 miles per hour (917 kmph), twice as fast as a racecar.

Emergency slides

If the plane has to land in an emergency, slides inflate so passengers can exit quickly.

Flight attendants look after the passengers.

The captain and the co-pilot sit in the **cockpit**.

The **weather radar system** spots any dangerous weather that may be on the way.

Jumbo jets use four special **jet engines** called turbofans.

This jumbo jet can fly over 6,835 miles (11,000 km) without stopping. That's farther than the California to Italy!

19

The Speed of Sound

Here are the fastest flying machines in the world. They can all travel at supersonic speeds—faster than the speed of sound! In air travel, the speed that sound travels is called Mach 1.

SUPER SONIC!

Lockheed SR-71 Blackbird
The Blackbird holds the world record for a piloted aircraft without a rocket engine. Imagine flying at 2,193 miles per hour (3,530 kmph), or **Mach 3.3**!

X-43A
This plane goes faster than all the rest, reaching **Mach 9.6**. It can't carry people and can only be used once. That doesn't sound very useful, but aircraft like this can teach us about the future of air travel.

Concorde

This was the first supersonic passenger plane. It could fly from London to New York in less than 3 hours at **Mach 2**.

When a plane reaches the speed of sound it creates a very loud noise called a sonic boom!

X-15

This is the fastest piloted plane ever, at **Mach 6.7**. It is powered by rocket jets and flies so high that the pilot needs an oxygen tank to breathe. No wonder they call it a space plane!

Sonic booms are more than twice as loud as thunder!

Sound can travel three soccer fields in one second!

Drone

A drone is an aircraft that doesn't need a pilot. These robotic flying machines are sometimes called UAVs—unmanned aerial vehicles. They can be controlled by computers or humans. How futuristic!

Here's a **multirotor drone**. It works like a mini helicopter. Cogz is flying it with a remote control.

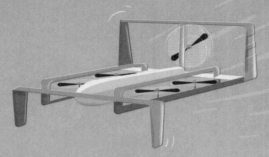

In the future your shopping might be delivered to your house by a **hybrid delivery drone** like this.

These buzzy little vehicles can carry small cameras. I can take photos from way up high! Smile!

This **weather drone** is packed with clever technology. It can predict when a storm might happen.

Jet Pack

Imagine being able to strap on a jet-powered backpack and zoom into the sky! Jet packs and rocket packs are not just science fiction. Real ones have been built for the army, for astronauts, and for spectacular stunt shows.

The Bell Rocket Belt

This rocket-powered backpack blasts hot steam out of rocket nozzles and can fly at 60 miles per hour (95 kmph), but only for 20 seconds.

what a blast!

The Bell Rocket Belt has been used in Hollywood action movies!

Jetman

Yves Rossy is an inventor also known as Jetman! He wears jet-powered wings to fly at over 100 miles per hour (160 kmph). In 2008 he flew across the English Channel and in 2011 he zoomed over the Grand Canyon.

Let's get our feet back on the ground! What have you learned on your journey?

Nutty and Bolt have come up with six questions. I'm sure you'll pass with flying colors!

1. Who invented the first successful airplane?

2. Where is jet fuel stored in an airplane?

3. What noise might you hear when an aircraft reaches the speed of sound?

4. Which aircraft can travel up, down, forward, and backward?

5. What is another name for an unmanned aerial vehicle?

6. Which is lighter, cold air or hot air?

Answers

1. The Wright Brothers, 2. In the wings, 3. A sonic boom, 4. A helicopter, 5. A drone, 6. Hot air